MW00443728

CHANTRY
CHOIRBOOK

SACRED MUSIC FOR ALL SEASONS

AUGSBURG FORTRESS
MINNEAPOLIS

Chantry Choirbook
Sacred Music for All Seasons

RELATED RESOURCES
Bach for All Seasons
Choirbook 0-8006-5854-X
Compact Disc 0-8006-5855-8

Copyright © 2000 Augsburg Fortress. All
rights reserved. Except for brief quotations in
critical articles or reviews, no part of this book
may be reproduced in any manner without
prior written permission from the publisher.
Write to: Permissions, Augsburg Fortress,
P.O. Box 1209, Minneapolis, MN 55440-1209.

General editor: Frank Stoldt
Editors: Carol Carver, Martin A. Seltz,
Christopher Sidorfsky, Eric Vollen
Music engraving: Thomas Schaller, Mensura
Music Preparation
Cover art: Nicholas Markell

The paper used in this publication meets the
minimum requirements of the American Na-
tional Standard for Information Sciences—
Permanence of Paper for Printed Materials,
ANSI Z39.48-1984.
Printed in the United States of America.

ISBN 0-8006-5777-2
12-114

17 18 19   11 10 9

CONTENTS

A rich and diverse tradition of choral singing among nations that share the German language has existed for close to one thousand years. Choir schools, singing academies, municipal *Kantorei*, parish choirs, and professional choral ensembles in Europe and beyond have inspired over five hundred years of choral literature created especially for performance within worship. Indeed, most of Europe's greatest composers since 1500 have contributed to this ever-expanding repertoire.

Many English-speaking countries, however, have had limited exposure to this music. Often the music is simply unavailable except in expensive, imported editions. A lack of high quality, singable English translations has also inhibited the music's potential use in worship. And finally, poorly prepared editions based on dated scholarship have discouraged conductors and choirs from adding this literature to their repertoire.

The goal of this *Chantry Choirbook*, then, is twofold: to provide present-day choirs with a compendium of the very best and most useful contributions of German choral music in singable English translations, and to encourage its performance within the context of the worshiping assembly. To that end, sixty selections extending over five centuries have been assembled in this volume.

The beginnings of the German choral school can be traced to the monastic foundations of the Middle Ages when monasteries supported choral foundations for the singing of the liturgy. These earliest choirs concentrated on singing plainsong (*Choral* in German) within the contexts of daily prayer and the Mass. By 1017, for example, Leipzig had a *Kapelle* at the Jacobskirche, and by 1212 the Thomaskirche (where Johann Sebastian Bach would become cantor in 1723) was established as a monastic institution, including a choir school. Up to the mid-fourteen hundreds, however, the bulk of repertoire for German choirs was unison *Choral*, with only minimal interest in the beginnings of polyphony. In addition, the vernacular religious folksong as well as the *Minnesang* and *Meistergesang* focused vocal music on the unison song. For centuries prior to the Reformation, therefore, unison Latin *Choral* and German folksong formed the basis of German vocal music; polyphony only began to enter common usage in the late fourteen hundreds.

By 1500, however, multi-voiced music in both Latin and German came into widespread use. This resulted partly from the invention of the movable type printing press, thus allowing broad distribution of part books. An equally important influence, however, was the musical consolidation around the year 1500 of the church, town, and royal court. Each town or royal court created musical establishments for the performance of both sacred and secular music.

GERMAN
CHORAL
TRADITION

Since 1500, there have been hundreds of composers who have expanded the German choral tradition with various motets, chorales, cantatas, oratorios, and passions. There are five composers, however, who stand out among the tradition's most influential shapers: Heinrich Schütz, Johann Sebastian Bach, Felix Mendelssohn, Johannes Brahms, and Hugo Distler. It is from these composers that this choirbook draws the greatest share of its repertoire.

Far more than any other composer, it was Heinrich Schütz (1585–1672) who refined the art of musical declamation for biblical text. *Kapellmeister* in Dresden (1617–1672) and twice a student of Giovanni Gabrieli in Venice, Schütz adapted Italian musical styles to the German language, and was especially influential in forming a new musical style in which the stresses of the spoken word drive the musical form. Even today his works form the basis of the repertoire of German choirs. His choral compositions range from massive polychoral motets to simple four-voice psalms to a cappella settings of the biblical

COMPOSERS

passions. The materials by him in this volume span close to forty years of his life and represent the variety of musical forms in which he wrote.

Felix Mendelssohn (1809–1847) was the most celebrated musician of his day, famous throughout Europe as well as North America. He was a renowned symphonic composer, conductor of the Leipzig Gewandhaus orchestra, and the choral conductor at the Berlin *Dom* and Singakademie. At age twenty, he revived Johann Sebastian Bach's *St. Matthew Passion* in Berlin. Later in life he organized the Leipzig conservatory with its famous school of church music. Mendelssohn's choral music is deeply influenced by his study of Bach and other early composers. The result is a rich melodic line combined with an older style counterpoint. Mendelssohn uplifts that chorale cantus firmus and uses it as a basis for various cantatas, motets, and oratorios.

A German by birth (in Hamburg in the Lutheran North) but Austrian by choice, Johannes Brahms (1833–1897) was a prodigious composer of symphonies, solo songs, and keyboard music. His sacred choral music represents a recovery of the conservative musical forms of the Renaissance and Baroque as well as a renewed interest in the chorale. Interestingly enough, his return to more orthodox textual and musical sources for his choral music parallels the German liturgical renewal of the mid-nineteenth century. For Roman Catholics, this recovery was centered at the Abbey of Maria Laach and its renewal of chant; for evangelical congregations it was focused in the school of Wilhelm Löhe at Neuendettelsau.

Hugo Distler (1908–1942) was a twentieth century composer, organist, and choral conductor active in Lübeck, Stuttgart, and Berlin. Distler is principally remembered by church musicians for his inventive combination of traditional chorale melodies, fluid Renaissance-style counterpoint, and stark, hollow harmonies. Distler tragically ended his life during the height of the Second World War.

The fifth composer is Johann Sebastian Bach (1685–1750). Throughout his life, Bach mastered both instrumental and choral music, as he worked for the royal court as well as several town governments. The breadth and substance of his work are so great, however, that a complete volume dedicated to his music has been prepared, separate from this collection, by Augsburg Fortress. Over forty selections from Bach's masses, passions, cantatas, and chorales are collected in *Bach for All Seasons*. Together, then, these two volumes provide a comprehensive sampling of the sacred choral works of five great composers.

From among the hundreds of other composers, several are represented in this collection and bear special mention. Josquin Desprez (c. 1440–1521) was a Franco-Flemish Renaissance composer who combined intricate Netherlandish counterpoint with the expressive art forms that formed a union of word and note. Martin Luther once stated that "Josquin is a master of the notes, which must express what he desires; on the other hand, other choral composers must do what the notes dictate." Josquin highly influenced the compositional techniques of German church music in the sixteenth century, thus resulting in a basic conservatism that set it apart from the more daring developments in Italy and France. Among the first leaders in German choral music was Johann Walter (1496–1570). As a close friend of Martin Luther, Walter assisted him in the evangelical reform of the Mass at Wittenberg in 1524. Walter also edited the *Geistliche Gesangbüchlein* (1524), the first published Lutheran hymnbook. He also served as *Kantor* (music director) in Torgau and *Kapellmeister* to the Elector of Saxony in Dresden.

Claude Goudimel (1510–1572) was a French Huguenot and a master of both French chanson and vernacular French psalmody. Serving in Metz, Besançon, and Lyons, Goudimel was a victim of the St. Bartholomew's Day massacres of 1572 that decimated the Huguenot population of Lyons. While not from a German principality, Goudimel and his psalm settings highlight French Protestant musical development that was happening at the time of Johann Walter. Gallus Dressler (1533–c. 1584) is principally remembered for his dramatic refinement of the German language biblical motet. Characteristically, Dressler's motets included highly developed musical text painting in which musical lines mirror the words of the text. Johannes Eccard (1553–1611) was a student of Lassus in Munich and served as *Kantor* in Augsburg, Königsberg, and Berlin. He is principally remembered for a large corpus of concerted chorale settings and motets. Jan Pieterszoon Sweelinck (1562–1621), a Dutch musician, was the most famous organist of his day, serving at the Oude Kerk in Amsterdam. His intricate keyboard counterpoint led to the development of the fugue. It was as a teacher, however, that he had the greatest influence on German choral music since among his students were Jakob Praetorius, Samuel Scheidt, and Heinrich Scheidemann.

Hans Leo Hassler (1564–1612) was a student of Andrea Gabrieli in Venice, and served as an organist and *Kantor* in Augsburg, Nürnberg, and Dresden. He is principally remembered for a fusion of the northern imitative style with the new Italian styles being developed in Venice. Melchior Vulpius (c. 1570–1615) was an influential hymn tune composer, serving as *Kantor* in Weimar. Michael Praetorius (1571–1621) was *Kantor* in Wolfenbüttel and Dresden, and created more than twelve hundred hymn settings for choirs, instruments, and congregations. Johann Crüger (1598–1662) was a Berlin composer and *Kantor* at Nicolaikirche, famous for his hymn tunes set with the texts of Paul Gerhardt. Dieterich Buxtehude (c. 1637–1707) was *Kantor* at the Marienkirche in Lübeck and was famous for his Abendmusik concerts. Composer of countless cantatas and organ works, Buxtehude's work had a direct influence on the young Johann Sebastian Bach. Johann Christoph Friedrich Bach (1732–1795) was the eldest surviving son of Johann Sebastian Bach and Anna Magdelena. While primarily a chamber musician in Bückburg, Johann Christoph's choral music tended to show characteristics of both his father's baroque traditionalism as well as the *Sturm und Drang* and classical form of the late eighteenth century.

EDITORIAL PRINCIPLES

Several editorial principles guided the preparation of this volume. The historical significance of various composers' choral music is reflected by the diverse selections that have been included. Biblical motets, chorale harmonizations, choral fugues, *stile antico* counterpoint, oratorio choruses, free-standing anthems, and contemporary motets represent the breadth of the repertoire's musical forms.

A concern for the pastoral usefulness suggested the inclusion of material that is congruent with current theological, homiletical, and sacramental emphases. Because the Lutheran tradition for which the majority of this repertoire was created understands music to be the *viva vox evangelii* (the living voice of the gospel), this collection was designed to support the church's ministry of proclamation through word and sacrament.

Selections were also chosen to support liturgical usage throughout the entire year within the context of the service of Holy Communion. A comprehensive set of lectionary, biblical, and topical indexes is included at the conclusion of the volume. These will assist choirs in singing from this volume throughout the changing seasons of the church year, as well as at the services of baptism, marriage, and burial.

Finally, the desire for the music's accessibility by parish choirs required that choices provide both a sense of achievement and challenge. Choirs with very limited resources can sing many of the smaller selections with confidence. More complex movements are included in order to provide choirs the opportunity to sing more ambitious excerpts.

TEXTS

The text for each movement is generally included in the original Latin or German version, and, in most cases, supported by an English translation suitable for singing. Because this repertoire extends over five centuries, slight discrepancies in style and spelling in the original sources will be noted.

English translations have been newly prepared or chosen from existing translations based on the following criteria:

- faithfulness to the meaning of the original German or Latin text
- congruence with a North American congregation's memory of these texts
- lyricism of the English poetry
- the worldview of the contemporary theological mind
- the musical demands of compositional structure, including selection of vowels for singing and the choice of text for repeated musical phrasing.

KEYBOARD
SCORES

A keyboard accompaniment for each selection has been newly prepared. In the case of music often sung a cappella, the keyboard score is a reduction of the vocal parts. For selections from the period of the musical Baroque (c. 1600–c. 1750), the keyboard score is generally treated as a *basso continuo;* in these cases, the bass line is the composer's original, but the harmonic structure has been realized by Layton James in a manner consistent with the style of the period as well as support needs of the singers. Other works included in this collection have an idiomatic organ accompaniment that has been crafted to be a careful transcription of independent orchestral scoring.

FOR
FURTHER
READING

Blume, Friedrich. *Protestant Church Music: A History.* New York: W. W. Norton, 1974.

For over fifty years, Chantry Music Press introduced the European church music revival to North American church musicians, scholars, and organ builders. From its founding in 1948 until his recent death, Frederick Martin Otto (1905–1999), the press's founder and primary creative spirit, was responsible for influencing generations of church musicians through his work as pastor, musicologist, and publisher.

Otto's lifelong interest in liturgy and music began at home in Detroit, Michigan. His father was a Thuringian pastor who had been educated at Wilhelm Löhe's school in Neuendettelsau, Germany, the center of evangelical liturgical revival in the mid-nineteenth century. In the 1920s, Frederick studied at the University of Leipzig with its famed Conservatory of Music and Institute for Church Music. In Leipzig Otto was a student of Karl Straube and Johannes Wolgast, as well as a singer in the Thomanerchor. It was also during these years that Otto became friends with Hugo Distler and Christoph Mahrenholz. In fact, it was through his friendship with Mahrenholz that Otto helped introduce the *Orgelbewegung* (organ revival movement) to North America through yet another acquaintance, Walter Holtkamp.

Chantry Music Press had its beginnings in 1948 in Fremont, Ohio, with the publication of Vincent Lübeck's *Christmas Cantata*. After the work was rejected by a Chicago publisher as having "no future in America," Otto relied upon Ulrich Leupold to prepare the work for publication and, with the help of his wife Georgia and a printing press in the garage of his church parsonage, Chantry Music Press was born. Over the next fifty years, Otto and Chantry Music Press would introduce over two hundred publications, including many by composers that have since become well-known in North America: Heinz Werner Zimmermann, Heinrich Schütz, Hugo Distler, Jan Bender, and Dieterich Buxtehude.

Chantry quickly became known for its careful musical scholarship and for its attention to engaging graphic design, artistic musical engraving, and elegant printing. Over the course of five decades, Otto continued to renew ties with church music leaders in Europe, and, as a result, organized church music workshops for many years in Berchtesgaden, Germany, as well as Lakeside, Ohio. In later years, Chantry moved to Springfield, Ohio, and enjoyed a particularly close relationship with Wittenberg University. In 1994, at age 89, Otto retired, and Augsburg Fortress acquired Chantry Music Press, with the mission to continue the publication of musical masterpieces from the European traditions.

It is with thanksgiving for the life, ministry, and publishing achievements of the Reverend Frederick Martin Otto that this *Chantry Choirbook* is dedicated.

Rise Up! Rise Up!

Wohlauf, wohlauf, mit hellem Ton

Johann Walter

© 2000 Augsburg Fortress

3

O Savior, Rend the Heavens Wide

O Heiland, reiss die Himmel auf

Hugo Distler

© 2000 Augsburg Fortress

Music © 1971 Bärenreiter-Verlag. Reprinted by permission. English text © 1969 Concordia Publishing House. Reprinted by permission.

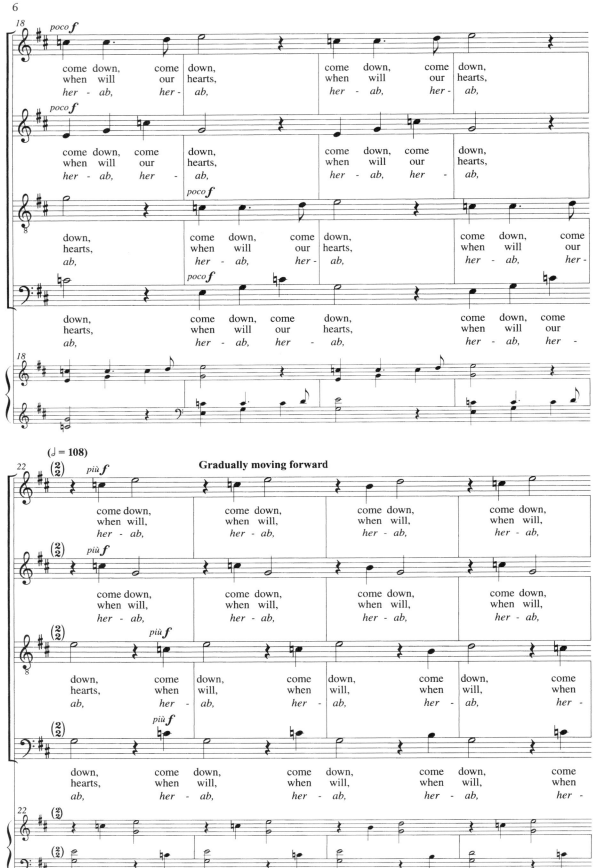

Very quick (Tempo II) 𝅗𝅥. = 72
p, ma cresc. sempre
Come down, come down, come down, come down,
when will our hearts, when will our hearts,
Her - ab, her - ab, her - ab, her - ab,
mp
mf
come down, come down, come down, come down,
when will our hearts, when will our hearts,
her - ab, her - ab, her - ab, her - ab,

My Soul Proclaims the Greatness of the Lord

Magnificat

Hans Leo Hassler

© 2000 Augsburg Fortress

A Dove Flew Down from Heaven

Es flog ein Täublein weiße

Johannes Brahms

© 2000 Augsburg Fortress

English text © 1971 Jaroslav J. Vajda. Reprinted by permission.

this is what God wish - es, this wish shall be my law.
life to dwell a - mong us, e - ter - nal God in - deed!

wish - es, this wish shall be my law. Yet more than
mong us, e - ter - nal God in - deed! This Je - sus

what God wish - es, this wish shall be my law. Yet
dwell a - mong us, e - ter - nal God in - deed! This

what God wish - es, this wish, my law. Yet
dwell a - mong us, e - ter - nal God! This

Yet more than will - ing I sur - rend - er
This Je - sus Christ - child, son whom Mar - y

will - ing, more than will - ing I sur - rend - er
Christ - child, Je - sus Christ - child, son whom Mar - y

more than will - ing I sur - rend - er me, if
Je - sus Christ - child, son whom Mar - y bore, is

more than will - ing I sur - rend - er me, if
Je - sus Christ - child, son whom Mar - y bore, is

Maria Walks Amid the Thorn

Maria durch ein' Dornwald ging

Hugo Distler

*All stanzas of this motet should be sung.

© 2000 Augsburg Fortress
Music © 1933 Bärenreiter-Verlag. Reprinted by permission.

Then Mary Said to the Angel

Dixit Maria ad angelum

Hans Leo Hassler

© 2000 Augsburg Fortress

24

Lo, How a Rose E'er Blooming

Es ist ein Ros entsprungen

Hugo Distler

© 2000 Augsburg Fortress
Music © 1948 Bärenreiter-Verlag. Reprinted by permission.

A Child to Us Is Born

Ein Kind ist uns geboren

Heinrich Schütz

An optional continuo part is included on p. 44.

© 2000 Augsburg Fortress

21
and do - min - ion rests up - on his
Wel - ches Herr - schaft ist auf sei - ner
ion rests up - on his shoul - der, and do - min - ion rests up - on his
schaft ist auf sei - ner Schul - ter, wel - ches Herr - schaft ist auf sei - ner
and do - min - ion rests up - on his
Wel - ches Herr - schaft ist auf sei - ner
rests up - on his shoul - der,
ist auf sei - ner Schul - ter,
rests up - on his shoul - der,
ist auf sei - ner Schul - ter,
26
shoul - der,
Schul - ter,
shoul - der,
Schul - ter,
shoul - der, and do - min - ion rests up - on his shoul -
Schul - ter, wel - ches Herr - schaft ist auf sei - ner Schul -
and do - min - ion, and do - min - ion rests up - on his shoul -
wel - ches Herr - schaft, wel - ches Herr - schaft ist auf sei - ner Schul -
and do - min - ion rests up - on his shoul -
wel - ches Herr - schaft ist auf sei - ner Schul -

A Child to Us Is Born

Ein Kind ist uns geboren

Optional
Continuo

© 2000 Augsburg Fortress

To Us Is Born Emmanuel

Enatus est Emanuel

Michael Praetorius

© 2000 Augsburg Fortress

48

50

Now to Us a Child Is Born

Heut ist uns ein Kindlein geborn

Hugo Distler

© 2000 Augsburg Fortress
Music © 1991 Bärenreiter-Verlag. Reprinted by permission.

52

Psallite

Michael Praetorius

© 2000 Augsburg Fortress

Raise a Song, Let Praise Abound

Resonet in laudibus

Johann Eccard

© 2000 Augsburg Fortress

There Shall a Star Come Out of Jacob

Es wird ein Stern aus Jacob aufgeh'n

Felix Mendelssohn

© 2000 Augsburg Fortress

64

66

74

O Morning Star, How Fair and Bright!

Wie schön leuchtet der Morgenstern

Michael Praetorius

A keyboard reduction is included on p. 82.
© 2000 Augsburg Fortress

80

O Morning Star, How Fair and Bright!

Wie schön leuchtet der Morgenstern

Michael Praetorius

Keyboard reduction
for rehearsal only

© 2000 Augsburg Fortress

In Peace and Joy I Now Depart

Mit Fried und Freud ich fahr dahin

Johannes Brahms

© 2000 Augsburg Fortress

For God So Loved the World

Also hat Gott die Welt geliebet

Hugo Distler

© 2000 Augsburg Fortress
Music © 1933 Bärenreiter-Verlag. Reprinted by permission.

Gradually calmer

God So Loved the World

Also hat Gott die Welt geliebt

Heinrich Schütz

© 2000 Augsburg Fortress

I Am the Resurrection and the Life

Ich bin die Auferstehung

Gallus Dressler

Anthem
Eb, Bb

© 2000 Augsburg Fortress

13
and ev - 'ry - one who lives and be - lieves in me, and ev - 'ry - one who lives and
und wer da le - bet und glau - bet an mich, und wer da le - bet und glau -
and ev - 'ry - one who lives and be - lieves in me, and ev - 'ry - one who lives and
und wer da le - bet und glau - bet an mich, und wer da le - bet und glau -
and ev - 'ry - one who lives and be - lieves in me, and ev - 'ry - one who lives and
und wer da le - bet und glau - bet an mich, und wer da le - bet und glau -
and ev - 'ry - one who lives and be - lieves in me, and ev - 'ry - one who lives and
und wer da le - bet und glau - bet an mich, und wer da le - bet und glau -
13
15
be - lieves in me, they will nev - er - more per -
bet an mich, der wird nim - mer - mehr ster -
be - lieves in me, they will nev - er - more per -
bet an mich, der wird nim - mer - mehr ster -
be - lieves in me, they will nev - er - more per -
bet an mich, der wird nim - mer - mehr ster -
be - lieves in me,
bet an mich,
15

Sing Hosanna to the Son of David

Hosianna dem Sohne Davids

Bartholomäus Gesius

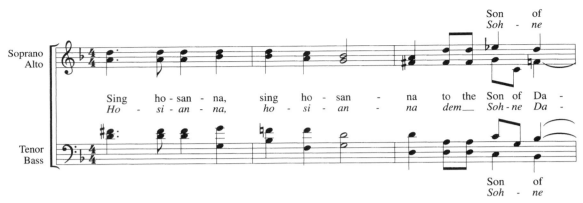

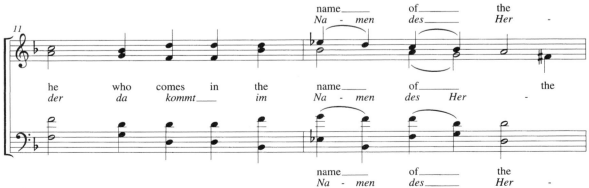

© 2000 Augsburg Fortress

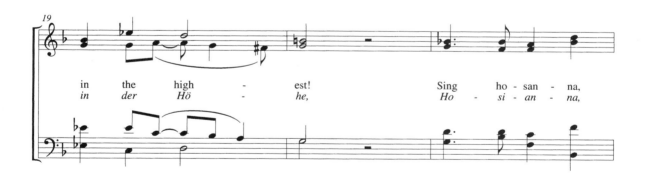

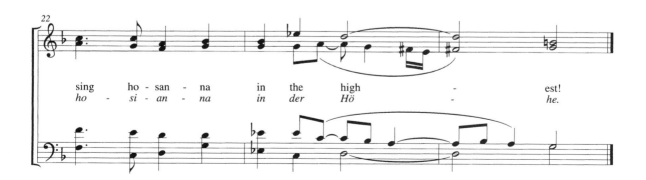

Ave verum corpus

Wolfgang Amadeus Mozart

Translation: Hail, true body, born of the Virgin Mary,
truly suffering, sacrificed on the cross for humanity,
whose side, when pierced, flowed with water and blood:
be for us a foretaste in death's agony.

© 2000 Augsburg Fortress

Praise to You, Lord Jesus

Ehre sei dir Christe

Heinrich Schütz

© 2000 Augsburg Fortress

A Lamb Goes Uncomplaining Forth

Ein Lämmlein geht und trägt die Schuld

Hugo Distler

© 2000 Augsburg Fortress
Music © 1987 Bärenreiter-Verlag. Reprinted by permission.

Today in Triumph Christ Arose

Heut triumphieret Gottes Sohn

Johann Crüger

Parts for C instruments are included on p. 116.
© 2000 Augsburg Fortress

sing e - ter - nal - ly. Al - le - lu - ia, al - le - lu - ia!
o - ver Sa - tan's fray. Al - le - lu - ia, al - le - lu - ia!
ihm in E - wig - keit. Hal - le - lu - jah, hal - le - lu - jah!

3 O blessed Jesus Christ, our Lord,
  who all the world from sin restored:
  alleluia, alleluia,
  with lovingkindness guide our ways
  that we may sing your endless praise.
  Alleluia, alleluia!

4 No foe can harm us evermore;
  death's murmurs are but ancient lore.
  Alleluia, alleluia!
  The evil one lies in the dust,
  but we are heirs to life robust.
  Alleluia, alleluia!

5 We offer thanks with heart and soul,
  and long to gain our heav'nly goal.
  Alleluia, alleluia!
  Help us to trust amid all doubt
  that we may sing with joyous shout:
  Alleluia, alleluia!

Today in Triumph Christ Arose

Heut triumphieret Gottes Sohn

Johann Crüger

C Instruments*

*Brass, woodwinds, or strings.

© 2000 Augsburg Fortress

Jesus Christ, My Sure Defense – Alleluia

Jesus, meine Zuversicht – Halleluja

Felix Mendelssohn

Je - sus Christ, my sure de - fense and my Sav - ior, ev - er liv - eth!
Je - sus, mei - ne Zu - ver - sicht, mein Er - lö - ser ist im Le - ben.

Know - ing this, my con - fi - dence rests up - on the hope it giv - eth,
Die - ses weiß ich; sollt' ich nicht mich dem To - de ganz er - ge - ben.

though the night of death be fraught still with man - y_an
Ob das Gras, das mich einst deckt, mein zu schwa - ches

anx - ious thought.
Herz er - schreckt?

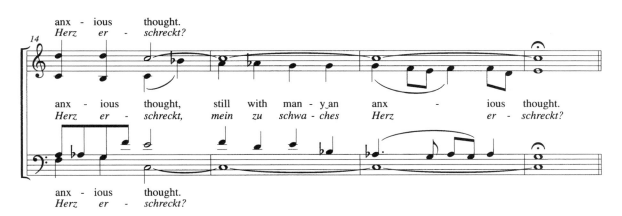

anx - ious thought, still with man - y_an anx - ious thought.
Herz er - schreckt, mein zu schwa - ches Herz er - schreckt?

anx - ious thought.
Herz er - schreckt?

© 2000 Augsburg Fortress

122

Awake, My Heart, with Gladness

Auf, auf, mein Herz, mit Freuden

Johann Crüger

Lyrics:

1 A - wake, my heart, with glad - ness, see
2 The foe in tri - umph shout - ed when
3 This is the sight that glad - dens— what

Auf, auf, mein Herz, mit Freu - den nimm

what to - day is done; now, af - ter
Christ lay in the tomb; but, lo, he
peace it does im - part! Now noth - ing

wahr, was heut ge - schicht; wie kommt nach

gloom and sad - ness, comes forth the
now is rout - ed, his boast is
ev - er sad - dens the joy with -

gro - ßem Lei - den nun ein so

© 2000 Augsburg Fortress

Measure 13:

glo - rious sun. My Sav - ior there was laid
turned to gloom. For Christ a - gain is free;
in my heart. No gloom shall ev - er shake,
gro - ßes Licht! Mein Hei - land war ge - legt,

Measure 18:

where our bed must be made when to the
in glo - rious vic - to - ry no foe shall ev - er take, the who is
no foe shall ev - er take, the hope which
da, wo man uns hin - trägt, wenn von uns

Measure 22:

realms of light our spir - it wings its flight.
strong to save has tri - umphed o'er the grave.
God's own Son in love for me has won.
un - ser Geist gen Him - mel ist ge - reist.

Stay with Us, Lord

Bleib bei uns, Herr

Michael Praetorius

© 2000 Augsburg Fortress

Arisen Is Our Blessed Lord

Erstanden ist der heilig Christ

Melchior Vulpius

4 Christ has arisen from the grave
alleluia, alleluia,
this holy day, our souls to save.
Alleluia, alleluia, alleluia, alleluia, alleluia, alleluia!

© 2000 Augsburg Fortress

135

5 Now let us sing without delay:
  alleluia, alleluia,
  the holy Christ is ris'n today.
  Alleluia, alleluia, alleluia, alleluia, alleluia!

6 Let all our joy rise full and free;
  alleluia, alleluia,
  our comfort Christ will ever be.
  Alleluia, alleluia, alleluia, alleluia, alleluia!

See God to Heaven Ascending

Gott fähret auf gen Himmel

Friedrich Samuel Riegel

1 See God to heav'n as-cend-ing in tri-umph to his throne,
2 Lo, heav'n with joy is sound-ing his glad re-turn to see;
Gott fäh-ret auf gen Him-mel mit fro-hem Ju-bel-schall,

great shouts of tu-mult blend-ing with trum-pets' thrill-ing tone!
be-hold the saints sur-round-ing the Lord who set them free;
mit präch-ti-gem Ge-tüm-mel und mit Po-sau-nen-hall.

Sing prais-es to your Lord! Sing prais-es, bring o-va-
now myr-iad an-gels come, the cher-ub band re-joic-
Lob-singt, lob-sin-get Gott! Lob-singt, lob-singt mit Freu-

tions, to Christ, the king of na-tions, the God of hosts a-dored!
es, and clear-est ser-aph voic-es all wel-come Je-sus home.
den dem Kö-ni-ge der Hei-den, dem Her-ren Ze-ba-oth!

3 We see the steps ascending that raised our Lord on high;
we see the highway wending to heav'n's unending joy.
Our Savior leads the way; yet he would not bereave us,
a well-marked path would leave us, prepares our passageway.

4 Let all our thoughts be winging, with you to heav'n ascend;
let all our hearts be singing: "We seek you, Savior, Friend,
God's own anointed Son, our life and way to heaven,
to whom all pow'r is given, our joy and hope and crown."

© 2000 Augsburg Fortress
English text © 1969 Concordia Publishing House. Reprinted by permission.

Creator Spirit, Heav'nly Dove

Komm, heiliger Geist, o Schöpfer du

Hugo Distler

© 2000 Augsburg Fortress
Music © 1933 Bärenreiter-Verlag. Reprinted by permission.

Come, Holy Ghost, God and Lord

Komm, Heiliger Geist, Herre Gott

Hugo Distler

Calm, but not slow

© 2000 Augsburg Fortress
Music © 1987 Bärenreiter-Verlag. Reprinted by permission.

O Spirit of God, Eternal Source

O Heiliger Geist, du ewiger Gott

Melchior Vulpius

1 O Spir - it of God, e - ter - nal source, with sev'n - fold
2 O Spir - it Di - vine, our com - fort true, in ev - 'ry
3 For - sak - ing your word, your gen - 'rous might, we wan - der
4 O Spir - it of God, most no - ble gift, send down your

O Hei - li - ger Geist, du e - wi - ger Gott, mit dei - nen

gifts to gov - ern life's course: stir up our souls, set us a -
need you strength - en, re - new; when an - y e - vil threat a -
paths of our own de - light; show us your love that we may
fire with vig - or so swift. Let end - less praise from us as -

Ga - ben steur uns - 'rer Not, auf dass wir Chris - tum, un - sern

blaze that we our Lord may faith - ful - ly praise.
larms give to us rest in your gra - cious arms.
see your grace and fa - vor e - ter - nal - ly. Ky - ri - e -
cend; on your sure prom - ise our lives de - pend.

Herrn, in rech - tem Glau - ben lie - ben und ehrn. Ky - ri - e -

le - i - son, Ky - ri - e - le - i - son.
le - i - son, Ky - ri - e - le - i - son.

© 2000 Augsburg Fortress

Salvation unto Us Has Come

Es ist das Heil uns kommen her

Hugo Distler

© 2000 Augsburg Fortress
Music © 1987 Bärenreiter-Verlag. Reprinted by permission.

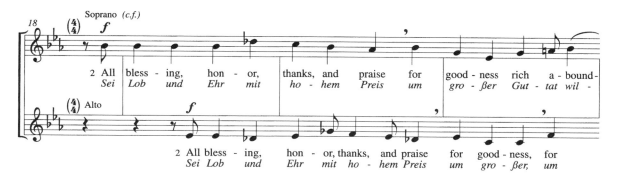

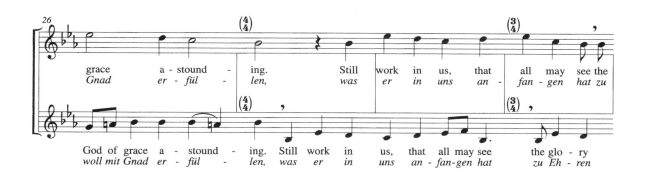

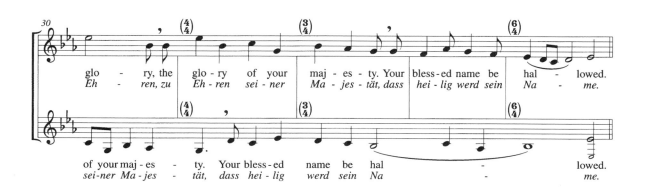

150

Even calmer

A Mighty Fortress Is Our God

Ein feste Burg ist unser Gott

Hans Leo Hassler

© 2000 Augsburg Fortress

159

162

I Build on God's Strong Word

Allein auf Gottes Wort

Johann Walther

Soprano: I build on God's strong word_____ se-
Al - lein auf Got - tes Wort_____ will

Alto: I build on God's strong word_____ se-
Al - lein auf Got - tes Wort_____ will

Tenor: I build on
Al - lein auf

for rehearsal only

Soprano: cure, on God's_____ strong word, the rock of
ich, auf Got - tes Wort will ich of mein

Alto: cure,_____ I build_____ on God's strong
ich,_____ al - lein auf Got - tes

Tenor: God's strong word_____ se -
Got - tes Wort_____ will

Bass: I build on God's strong word_____ se -
Al - lein auf Got - tes Wort_____ will

© 2000 Augsburg Fortress

168

In the Resurrection Glorious

In der Auferstehung Gottes

Johann Christoph Friedrich Bach

© 2000 Augsburg Fortress

172

178

They That Shall Endure to the End

Wer bis an das Ende beharrt

Felix Mendelssohn

© 2000 Augsburg Fortress

An earlier English translation ("He that shall endure to the end shall be saved") was prepared by William Bartholomew based on the King James Bible. The current translation reflects more closely the German text.

O World So Vain

Ach, arme Welt

Johannes Brahms

© 2000 Augsburg Fortress

How Lovely Is Thy Dwellingplace

Wie lieblich sind deine Wohnungen

Johannes Brahms

© 2000 Augsburg Fortress

The Blood of Jesus Christ

Das Blut Jesu Christi

Heinrich Schütz

The blood / Das Blut

The blood of Je-sus Chris-sus / Das Blut Je-su Chris-ti

of Je-sus Chris-ti / Je-su Chris-ti

Christ, / ti

Christ, the bless-ed Son of / ti des Soh-nes Got -

the bless-ed Son / des Soh-nes Got -

God, wash-es a-way our ev-'ry, our ev-'ry, our ev- / tes, ma-chet uns rein von al-len, von al-len, von al-

© 2000 Augsburg Fortress

6

Soul, Adorn Yourself with Gladness

Schmücke dich, o liebe Seele

Friedrich Zipp

1 Soul, a - dorn your - self with glad - ness, leave the gloom - y haunts of sad - ness.
Come in - to the day - light's splen - dor, there with joy your prais - es ren - der.
Bless the one whose grace un - bound - ed this a - maz - ing ban - quet found - ed; he though heav'n - ly high and

3 Je - sus, source of last - ing plea - sure, tru - est friend and dear - est trea - sure,
peace be - yond all un - der - stand - ing, joy in - to all life ex - pand - ing:
hum - bly now, I bow be - fore you, Love in - car - nate, I a - dore you; wor - thi - ly let me re -

*The ritornell should be played before stanza one, between stanzas, and at the conclusion. It is scored for two violins or other C instruments, and cello. The ritornell could also be played on a keyboard.

© 2000 Augsburg Fortress
Music © 1956 Bärenreiter-Verlag. Reprinted by permission.

O Bread of Life from Heaven

O esca viatorum

Heinrich Isaac

for rehearsal only

© 2000 Augsburg Fortress

O Mighty Word of God Come Down

Verbum supernum prodiens

Josquin Desprez

3 Your holy body and your blood
were giv'n that life might spring and bud;
in bread and cup we share the feast
of you, O Christ, our great high priest.

4 In life you bore our human frame,
feeding the hungry, lost, and lame.
In death you knew our harsh demise;
you live and reign: grant us the prize.

A keyboard reduction is included on p. 216.

© 2000 Augsburg Fortress

came with us_____ to_____ dwell, to work till
self as liv - ing_____ bread at your dis -
su - um ex - i - ens, ve - nit ad

came with us to dwell, to work till
self as liv - ing bread at your dis -
su - um ex - i - ens, ve - nit_____ ad_____

you came with us_____ to_____ dwell, to work
your - self as liv - ing_____ bread at your
pus su - um ex - i - ens, ve - nit

came with us to dwell, to work till
self as liv - ing bread at your dis -
su - um ex - i - ens, ve - nit ad

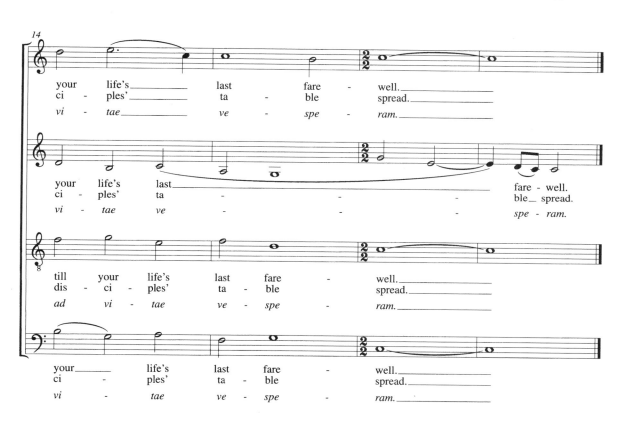

your life's_____ last fare - well._____
ci - ples'_____ ta - ble spread._____
vi - tae_____ ve - spe - ram._____

your life's last_____ fare - well.
ci - ples' ta - ble_ spread.
vi - tae ve - spe - ram.

till your life's last fare - well._____
dis - ci - ples' ta - ble spread._____
ad vi - tae ve - spe - ram._____

your_____ life's last fare - well._____
ci - ples' ta - ble spread._____
vi - tae ve - spe - ram._____

5 Great Paschal Lamb, our sacrifice:
  fling wide the door to paradise;
  when foes surround this earthly life
  give strength, give hope in time of strife.

6 All praise to you, blest One in Three,
  now and through all eternity!
  Bring us at last when life is spent
  to heaven's final sacrament.

O Mighty Word of God Come Down

Verbum supernum prodiens

Josquin Desprez

Keyboard reduction

for rehearsal only

© 2000 Augsburg Fortress

All My Spirit Longs to Savor

Ach wie hungert mein Gemüte

Georg Frideric Handel

1 All my spirit longs to savor, dearest Friend, your grace and favor. Oh, how deeply
2 Jesus, source of lasting pleasure, truest friend, and dearest treasure, peace beyond all

Ach wie hungert mein Gemüte, Menschenfreund, nach deiner Güte! Ach wie pfleg ich

© 2000 Augsburg Fortress

Let Grief Not Overwhelm You

Lass dich nur nichts nicht dauren

Johannes Brahms

© 2000 Augsburg Fortress

224

228

How Lovely Are the Messengers

Wie lieblich sind die Boten

Felix Mendelssohn

© 2000 Augsburg Fortress

233

Everything You Do

Alles was ihr tut

Dieterich Buxtehude

SONATA

© 2000 Augsburg Fortress

TUTTI

repeat SONATA

We Offer Our Thanks

Dank sagen wir alle Gott

Heinrich Schütz

Soprano
Alto

Tenor
Bass

Optional
Continuo

We of-fer our thanks and praise to our Lord Je - sus Christ, who with his
Dank sa - gen wir al - le Gott un-serm Her - ren Chri - sto, der uns mit

won - d'rous word has en - light - ened us, and has re - deemed us by his blood and pas -
sei - nem Wort hat er - leuch - tet und uns er - lö - set hat mit sei - nem Blu -

sion from the dev - il's grasp, from the dev - il's grasp. Then
te von des Teu - fels Gwalt, von des Teu - fels Gwalt. Den

© 2000 Augsburg Fortress

Grant Peace, We Pray
Verleih uns Frieden gnädiglich

Felix Mendelssohn

Grant peace, we pray, in mer- cy, Lord; in our time
Ver - leih uns Frie - den gnä - dig - lich, Herr Gott, zu

© 2000 Augsburg Fortress

254

On God Alone My Hope I Build

Auf Gott allein will hoffen ich

Felix Mendelssohn

© 2000 Augsburg Fortress

Now All the Woods Are Sleeping

Nun ruhen alle Wälder

Hugo Distler

© 2000 Augsburg Fortress
Music © 1998 Bärenreiter-Verlag. Reprinted by permission.

Praise to the Lord, the Almighty

Lobe den Herren, den mächtigen König der Ehren

Hugo Distler

© 2000 Augsburg Fortress
Music © 1987 Bärenreiter-Verlag. Reprinted by permission.

Sing to the Lord

Singet dem Herrn ein neues Lied

Heinrich Schütz

4 Sound all the drums, the trumpets blast,
praising our God, the first and last,
LORD evermore, life's origin.
Sing, crashing sea, and all therein!

5 Ends of the earth, God's glory show;
all living things, let praises grow.
Rapids and rivers, clap and roar;
mountains and hills, let triumph soar.

6 All this be done before the LORD,
who comes to judge with mighty word.
God's ev'ry deed confirms the right;
justice for all is God's delight.

© 2000 Augsburg Fortress

Sing to the Lord, New Songs Be Raising

Chantez à Dieu chanson nouvelle

Jan Pieterszoon Sweelinck

© 2000 Augsburg Fortress

21

tell   of God's great deeds a - maz - ing, and tell   of God's   great
de - li - vran - ce so - lem - nel - le, sa de - li - vran - ce

of God's great deeds   a - maz - ing, and tell   of God's great
li - vran - ce so - lem - nel - le, sa de - li - vran - ce

tell of God's great deeds a - maz - ing,   and tell of God's great
de - li - vran - ce so - lem - nel - le,   sa de - li - vran - ce

of God's great deeds a - maz - ing, and tell   of God's great
- li - vran - ce so - lem - nel - le, sa de - li - vran - ce

23   **1**   **2**

deeds a - maz - ing.   Sing ing, deeds   a - maz - ing.
so - lem - nel - le.   Chan le, so - lem - nel - le.

deeds a - maz - ing.   Sing ing, deeds a - maz - ing.
so - lem - nel - le.   Chan le, so - lem - nel - le.

deeds a - maz - ing. Sing out,   ing, deeds   a - maz - ing.
so - lem - nel - le. Chan - tez,   le, so - lem - nel - le.

deeds a - maz - ing.   Sing ing, deeds   a - maz - ing.
so - lem - nel - le.   Chan le, so - lem - nel - le.

As the Deer, for Water Yearning

Ainsi qu'on oit le cerf bruire

Claude Goudimel

© 2000 Augsburg Fortress

O Lord, I Trust Your Shepherd Care

Der Herr ist mein getreuer Hirt

Heinrich Schütz

© 2000 Augsburg Fortress

The alternate accompaniment is intended for a solo singer or unison section. One option would be to perform verse 1 with a soloist and this accompaniment, verse 2 SATB a cappella, and verse 3 SATB with the accompaniment that appears with the choral parts.

Lift Up Your Voice

Lobt Gott mit Schall

Heinrich Schütz

© 2000 Augsburg Fortress

Cantate Domino canticum novum

Hans Leo Hassler

Translation: Sing to the LORD a new song, sing to the LORD all the earth.
Sing to the LORD and bless his name.
Announce from day to day his salvation.
Announce among the nations his glory,
among all the peoples his wonders.

© 2000 Augsburg Fortress

Kyrie

Hans Leo Hassler

Translation: Lord, have mercy. Christ, have mercy. Lord, have mercy.

© 2000 Augsburg Fortress

Agnus Dei

Hans Leo Hassler

Translation: Lamb of God, you take away the sins of the world, have mercy on us.
Lamb of God, you take away the sins of the world, have mercy on us.
Lamb of God, you take away the sins of the world, grant us peace.

© 2000 Augsburg Fortress

Our Father

Vater unser

Heinrich Schütz

© 2000 Augsburg Fortress

ACKNOWLEDGMENTS

"A Child to Us Is Born" ("Ein Kind ist uns geboren"). Composer: Heinrich Schütz (1585–1672). Source: Geistliche Chormusik (1648), SWV 384. Text: Isaiah 9:6-7; tr. Frank Stoldt (b. 1958), © 2000 Augsburg Fortress. Continuo realization: Layton James (b. 1941), © 2000 Augsburg Fortress.

"A Dove Flew Down from Heaven" ("Es flog ein Täublein weiße"). Composer: Johannes Brahms (1833–1987). Source: Deutsche Volkslieder I (1864). Tune: ES FLOG EIN TÄUBLEIN WEIßE, Medieval German Leise (c. 1400). Text: D.G. Corner, Groß-Catolisch Gesangbuch (1631); tr. Jaroslav J. Vajda (b. 1919), © 1971 Jaroslav J. Vajda. Used by permission.

"A Lamb Goes Uncomplaining Forth" ("Ein Lämmlein geht und trägt die Schuld"). Composer: Hugo Distler (1908–1942), © 1987 Bärenreiter-Verlag, Kassel. Reprinted by permission. Source: "Fürwaht, er trug unsere Krankheit" in Geistliche Chormusik (1941), Opus 12, no. 9. Tune: AN WASSERFLÜSSEN BABYLON, Wolfgang Dachstein (c. 1487–1533). Text: Paul Gerhardt (1607–1676); tr. Lutheran Book of Worship, © 1978.

"A Mighty Fortress Is Our God" ("Ein feste Burg ist unser Gott"). Composer: Hans Leo Hassler (1564–1612). Source: Psalmen und Christliche Gesänge (1607). Tune: EIN FESTE BURG IST UNSER GOTT, Martin Luther (1483–1546). Text: Martin Luther (1483–1546); tr. Lutheran Book of Worship, © 1978.

"Agnus Dei." Composer: Hans Leo Hassler (1564–1612). Source: "Missa Secunda," Missae (1599). Text: Latin hymn (c. 900).

"All My Spirit Longs to Savor" ("Ach wir hungert mein Gemüte") Composer: Georg Frideric Händel (1685–1759). Source: Brockes Passion (1716). Tune: SCHMÜCKE DICH, Johann Crüger (1598–1662). Text: Johann Franck (1618–1677); tr. st. 1, Martin A. Seltz (b. 1951), © 2000 Augsburg Fortress. Organ transcription: Bruce Bengtson (b. 1953), © 2000 Augsburg Fortress.

"Arisen Is Our Blessed Lord" ("Erstanden ist der heilig Christ"). Composer: Melchior Vulpius (c. 1570–1615). Source: Erster Theil deutscher sontäglicher evangelischen Sprüche von Advent bis auff Trinitatis (1612). Tune: ERSTANDEN IST DER HEILIG CHRIST, fourteenth century; Höhenfurt (1410); Böhmische Brüder (1501/1531). Text: Böhmische Brüder, Nürnberg (1544); based on "Surrexit Christus hodie" (c. 1250); tr. Frank Stoldt (b. 1958), © 2000 Augsburg Fortress.

"As the Deer, for Water Yearning" ("Ainsi qu'on oit le cerf bruire"). Composer: Claude Goudimel (1510–1572). Source: Les sent cinquante Pseaumes de David (1568). Tune: FREU DICH SEHR, adapted by Louis Bourgeois in Trente quatre pseaumes de David, Geneva (1551), based on the French folksong "Ne l'oseray je dire" (1505). Text: Théodore de Bèze (1519–1605); tr. Frank Stoldt (b. 1958) and Martin A. Seltz (b. 1951), © 2000 Augsburg Fortress.

"Ave verum corpus." Composer: Wolfgang Amadeus Mozart (1756–1791). Source: KV618. Text: attr. to Pope Innocent III (1198–1216) or Pope Innocent IV (1243–1254). Organ transcription: Frank Stoldt (b. 1958), © 2000 Augsburg Fortress.

"Awake, My Heart, with Gladness" ("Auf, auf, mein Herz, mit Freuden"). Composer: Johann Crüger (1598–1662). Source: Geistliche Kirchenmelodien (1649). Tune: AUF, AUF, MEIN HERZ, Johann Crüger (1598–1662). Text: Paul Gerhardt (1607–1676); tr. Lutheran Book of Worship, © 1978.

"Cantate Domino canticum novum." Composer: Hans Leo Hassler (1564–1612). Source: Sacri concentus quator editio nova (1612). Text: Psalm 96:1-3 (Vulgate).

"Come, Holy Ghost, God and Lord" ("Komm, Heiliger Geist, Herre Gott"). Composer: Hugo Distler (1908–1942), © 1987 Bärenreiter-Verlag, Kassel. Reprinted by permission. Source: Kleine Choralmotetten für vierstimmigen gemischten Chor (1933), Opus 6/II. Tune: KOMM, HEILIGER GEIST, HERRE GOTT, Enchiridion, Erfurt (1524). Text: Martin Luther (1483–1546); tr. The Lutheran Hymnal (1941).

"Creator Spirit, Heavenly Dove" ("Komm, Heilger Geist, o Schöpfer du"). Composer: Hugo Distler (1908–1942), © 1933 Bärenreiter-Verlag, Kassel. Reprinted by permission. Source: Der Jahrkreis (1933), Opus 5. Tune: VENI CREATOR SPIRITUS, Kempten (c. 1000). Text: attr. Rhabanus Maurus (776–856); tr. Lutheran Book of Worship © 1978.

"Everything You Do" ("Alles was ihr tut"). Composer: Dieterich Buxtehude (c. 1637–1707). Source: Alles, was ihr tut (c. 1675), BuxWV4. Text: Colossians 3:17; tr. Mark P. Bangert (b. 1938), © 2000 Augsburg Fortress. Organ transcription: Frank Stoldt (b. 1958), © 2000 Augsburg Fortress.

"For God So Loved the World" ("Also hat Gott die Welt geliebt"). Composer: Hugo Distler (1908–1942), © 1933 Bärenreiter-Verlag, Kassel. Reprinted by permission. Source: Der Jahrkreis (1933), Opus 5. Text: John 3:16; tr. Martin A. Seltz (b. 1951), © 2000 Augsburg Fortress.

"God So Loved the World" ("Also hat Gott die Welt geliebt"). Composer: Heinrich Schütz (1585–1672). Source: Geistliche Chormusik (1648), SWV 380. Text: John 3:16; tr. Martin A. Seltz (b. 1951), © 2000 Augsburg Fortress. Continuo realization: Layton James (b. 1941), © 2000 Augsburg Fortress.

"Grant Peace, We Pray" ("Verleih uns Frieden gnädiglich"). Composer: Felix Mendelssohn (1809–1847). Text: Medieval antiphon; adapted Martin Luther (1483–1546); tr. Laudamus, © 1952 Lutheran World Federation. Organ transcription: Frank Stoldt (b. 1958), © 2000 Augsburg Fortress.

"How Lovely Are the Messengers" ("Wie lieblich sind die Boten"). Composer: Felix Mendelssohn (1809–1847). Source: Paulus (1836), Opus 36. Text: Romans 10:15; tr. William Bartholomew (1793–1867). Organ transcription: Frank Stoldt (b. 1958), © 2000 Augsburg Fortress.

"How Lovely Is Thy Dwellingplace" ("Wie lieblich sind deine Wohnungen"). Composer: Johannes Brahms (1833–1897). Source: Ein deutsches Requiem (1868), Opus 45. Text: Psalm 84:2-3, 5; tr. composite. Organ transcription: Frank Stoldt (b. 1958), © 2000 Augsburg Fortress.

"I Am the Resurrection" ("Ich bin die Auferstehung"). Composer: Gallus Dressler (1533–c. 1584). Source: XVI Gesang, Magdeburg (1570). Text: John 1:25-26; tr. composite, © 2000 Augsburg Fortress.

"I Build on God's Strong Word" ("Allein auf Gottes Wort"). Composer: Johann Walter (1496–1570). Source: Das Christlich Kinderlied D Martini Lutheri, Wittenberg (1566). Tune: Johann Walter (1496–1570). Text: Johann Walter (1496–1570); tr. Martin A. Seltz (b. 1951), © 2000 Augsburg Fortress.

"In Peace and Joy I Now Depart" ("Mit Fried und Freud"). Composer: Johannes Brahms (1833–1897). Source: Zwei Motteten (1879), Opus 74, no. 1. Tune: MIT FRIED UND FREUD, Martin Luther (1483–1546). Text: Martin Luther (1483–1546); tr. composite, © 2000 Augsburg Fortress.

"In the Resurrection Glorious" ("In der Auferstehung Gottes"). Composer: Johann Christoph Friedrich Bach (1732–1795). Source: Die Auferweckung Lazarus (1773). Text: Johann Gottfried Herder (1744–1803); tr. Frank Stoldt (b. 1958), © 2000 Augsburg Fortress. Organ transcription: Frank Stoldt (b. 1958), © 2000 Augsburg Fortress.

"Jesus Christ, My Sure Defense—Alleluia" ("*Jesu, meine Zuversicht—Halleluja*"). Composer: Felix Mendelssohn (1809–1847). Tune: JESUS, MEINE ZUVERSICHT, Johann Crüger (1598–1662). Text: Berlin (1653); tr. Catherine Winkworth (1829–1878).

"Kyrie." Composer: Hans Leo Hassler (1564–1612). Source: "Missa Secunda," *Missae* (1599). Text: Greek litany.

"Let Grief Not Overwhelm You" ("*Lass dich nur nichts nicht dauren*"). Composer: Johannes Brahms (1833–1897). Source: *Geistliches Lied* (1856), Opus 30. Text: Paul Flemming (1609–1640); tr. Martin A. Seltz (b. 1951), © 2000 Augsburg Fortress.

"Lift Up Your Voice" ("*Lobt Gott mit Schall ihr Heiden all*"). Composer: Heinrich Schütz (1585–1672). Source: *Psalmen Davids in Teutzchen Reimen gebracht durch D. Cornelius Berkern* (1628), SWV 215. Text: Cornelius Becker (1561–1604); tr. Frank Stoldt (b. 1958), © 2000 Augsburg Fortress. Continuo realization: Layton James (b. 1941), © 2000 Augsburg Fortress.

"Lo, How a Rose E'er Blooming" ("*Es ist ein Ros entsprungen*"). Composer: Hugo Distler (1908–1942), © 1948 Bärenreiter-Verlag, Kassel. Reprinted by permission. Source: *Die Weihnachtsgeschichte* (1933), Opus 10. Tune: ES IST EIN ROS, Köln (1599). Text: Mainz (1585); tr. Theodore Baker (1851–1934).

"Maria Walks Amid the Thorn" ("*Maria durch ein' Dornwald ging*"). Composer: Hugo Distler (1908–1942), © 1933 Bärenreiter-Verlag, Kassel. Reprinted by permission. Source: *Der Jahrkreis* (1933), Opus 5. Tune: MARIA DURCH EIN' DORNWALD GING, Medieval German *Leise* (c. 1400). Text: German folk carol; tr. Henry S. Drinker (1880–1965).

"My Soul Proclaims the Greatness of the Lord" ("*Magnificat*"). Composer: Hans Leo Hassler (1564–1612). Source: *Kirchengesänge: Psalmen und geistliche Lieder, auff die gemeinen Melodeyen* (1608). Tune: *Tonus Peregrinus* ("wandering tone"), Medieval psalm tone (c. 850). Text: Luke 1:46-55; tr. English Language Liturgical Consultation, © 1988.

"Now All the Woods Are Sleeping " ("*Nun ruhen alle Wälder*"). Composer: Hugo Distler (1908–1942), © 1998 Bärenreiter-Verlag, Kassel. Reprinted by permission. Tune: INNSBRUCK ICH MUß DICH LASSEN, German folk melody (c. 1425). Text: Paul Gerhardt (1607–1676); tr. *Lutheran Book of Worship*, © 1978, based on Catherine Winkworth (1829–1878).

"Now to Us a Child Is Born" ("*Heut ist uns ein Kindlein geborn*"). Composer: Hugo Distler (1908–1942), © 1991 Bärenreiter-Verlag, Kassel. Reprinted by permission. Text: Martin Luther (1483–1546); tr. Martin A. Seltz (b. 1951), © 2000 Augsburg Fortress.

"O Bread of Life from Heaven" ("*O esca viatorum*"). Composer: Heinrich Isaac (c. 1450–1517). Source: Georg Forster, *Frische teutsche Lieder*, Nürnberg (1539). Tune: INNSBRUCK ICH MUß DICH LASSEN, German folk melody (c. 1425). Text: Würzburg (1649); tr. *Lutheran Book of Worship*, © 1978, based on Philip Schaff (1819–1893) and Hugh Thomas Henry (1862–1946).

"O Lord, I Trust Your Shepherd Care" ("*Der Herr ist mein getreuer Hirt*"). Composer: Heinrich Schütz (1585–1672). Source: *Psalmen Davids in Teutzchen Reimen gebracht durch D. Cornelius Berkern* (1628), SWV 120. Text: Cornelius Becker (1561–1604); tr. Martin A. Seltz (b. 1951), © 2000 Augsburg Fortress. Continuo realization: Layton James (b. 1941), © 2000 Augsburg Fortress.

"O Mighty Word of God Come Down" ("*Verbum supernum prodiens*"). Composer: Josquin Desprez (c. 1440–1521). Source: *Ave Maria, gratia plena...virgo serena*. Text: Thomas Aquinas (1277–1274); tr. Frank Stoldt (b. 1958), © 2000 Augsburg Fortress.

"O Morning Star, How Fair and Bright" ("*Wie schön leuchtet der Morgenstern*"). Composer: Michael Praetorius (1571–1621). Source: *Musae Sioniae VIII* (1610). Tune: WIE SCHÖN LEUCHTET DER MORGENSTERN, Philipp Nicolai (1556–1608). Text: Philipp Nicolai (1556–1608); tr. *Lutheran Book of Worship*, © 1978.

"O Savior, Rend the Heavens Wide" ("*O Heiland, reiß die Himmel auf*"). Composer: Hugo Distler (1908–1942), © 1971 Bärenreiter-Verlag, Kassel. Reprinted by permission. Tune: O HEILAND, REIß DIE HIMMEL AUF, Croner Gesangbuch (1631). Text: Friedrich Spee (1591–1635); tr. Martin L. Seltz (1909–1967), © 1969 Concordia Publishing House.

"O Spirit of God, Eternal Source" ("*O Heilger Geist, du ewiger Gott*"). Composer: Melchior Vulpius (c. 1570–1615). Source: *Kirchen Geseng und geistliche Lieder* (1609). Tune: O HEILIGER GEIST, DU EWIGER GOTT, Melchior Vulpius (c. 1570–1615). Text: Bartholomäus Helder (c. 1585–1635); tr. Frank Stoldt (b. 1958), © 2000 Augsburg Fortress.

"O World So Vain" ("*Ach, arme Welt*"). Composer: Johannes Brahms (1833–1897). Source: *Drei Motteten* (1890), Opus 110, no. 2. Text: Ancient church hymn; tr. Martin A. Seltz (b. 1951), © 2000 Augsburg Fortress.

"On God Alone My Hope I Build" ("*Auf Gott allein will hoffen ich*"). Composer: Felix Mendelssohn (1809–1847). Source: *Aus tiefer Not schrei ich zu dir* (1830), Opus 23, no. 1. Text: Martin Luther (1483–1546); tr. Martin A. Seltz (b. 1951), © 2000 Augsburg Fortress.

"Our Father" ("*Vater unser*"). Composer: Heinrich Schütz (1585–1672). Source: *Zwölf Geistliche Gesänge* (1657), SWV 429. Text: Matthew 6:9-13; tr. Martin A. Seltz (b. 1951), © 2000 Augsburg Fortress). Continuo realization: Layton James (b. 1941), © 2000 Augsburg Fortress.

"Praise to the Lord, the Almighty" ("*Lobe den Herren, den mächtigen König der Ehren*"). Composer: Hugo Distler (1908–1942), © 1987 Bärenreiter-Verlag, Kassel. Reprinted by permission. Source: *Kleine Choralmotetten für vierstimmigen gemischten Chor* (1933), Opus 6/II. Tune: LOBE DEN HERRN, seventeenth-c; *Ernewerten Gesangbuch*, Stralsund (1665); Halle 1741. Text: Joachim Neander (1650–1680); tr. Martin A. Seltz (b. 1951), © 2000 Augsburg Fortress.

"Praise to You, Lord Jesus" ("*Ehre sei dir Christe*"). Composer: Heinrich Schütz (1585–1672). Source: *Historia des Leidens und Sterbens unsers Herrn und Heyland Jesu Christi noch dem Evangelisten S. Matheum* (1666), SWV 479. Text: Medieval trope of Latin liturgical text *Laus tibi, Christe* (c. 1300); German hymn by Konrad Michael von Nordhausen (1560); tr. composite, © 2000 Augsburg Fortress. Continuo realization: Layton James (b. 1941), © 2000 Augsburg Fortress.

"Psallite." Composer: Michael Praetorius (1571–1621). Source: *Musae Sioniae VI* (1609). Music: Anonymous French chanson; *Trente et Six Chansons musicales*, Paris (1530). Text: Anonymous macaronic Latin/German hymn (c. 1500); *Catholische geistliche Gesäng* (1608); tr. Martin A. Seltz (b. 1951), © 2000 Augsburg Fortress.

"Raise a Song, Let Praise Abound" ("*Resonet in laudibus*"). Composer: Johannes Eccard (1553–1611). Source: *Der erste Theil Geistlicher Lieder auff den Choral oder gemeine Kirchen-Melodey...mit fünff Stimmen componiret durch Johannem Eccardum Mulhusinum*, Königsberg (1597). Tune: RESONET IN LAUDIBUS, Moosburg Gradual (c. 1355); St. Gall manuscript (c. 1450). Text: *Catholische Cantual*, Mainz (1605); tr. Martin A. Seltz (b. 1951), © 2000 Augsburg Fortress.

"Rise Up, Rise Up!" ("*Wohlauf, wohlauf mit hellem Ton*"). Composer: Johann Walter (1496–1570). Source: *Geistliche Gesangbüchlein*, Wittenberg (1551). Tune: *Reuterliedlein*, Frankfurt an Main (1535). Text: Johann Walter (1496–1570), alt.; tr. Frank Stoldt (b. 1958), © 2000 Augsburg Fortress.

"Salvation unto Us Has Come" ("Es ist das Heil uns kommen her"). Composer: Hugo Distler (1908–1942), © 1987 Bärenreiter-Verlag, Kassel. Reprinted by permission. Source: *Kleine Choralmotetten für vierstimmigen gemischten Chor* (1933), Opus 6/II. Tune: ES IST DAS HEIL UNS KOMMEN HER, *Etlich christlich Lieder*, Wittenberg (1524); based on German hymn "Freu dich, du werthe Christenheit," Mainz (c. 1390). Text: Paul Speratus (1481–1551), tr. *Evangelical Lutheran Hymn-Book* (1912) and Martin A. Seltz (b. 1951), © 2000 Augsburg Fortress.

"See God to Heaven Ascending" ("Gott fähret auf gen Himmel"). Composer: Friedrich Samuel Riegel (1825–1907). Source: *Musica Sacra*, Göttingen (1869, 1895). Tune: ZEUCH EIN ZU DEINEN TOREN, Johann Crüger (1598–1662). Text: Gottfried W. Sacer (1635–1699); tr. Martin L. Seltz (1909–1967), © 1969 Concordia Publishing House.

"Sing Hosanna to the Son of David" ("Hosianna dem Sohne Davids"). Composer: Bartholomäus Gesius (c. 1555–1613). Source: *Enchiridium Etlicher Deutschen und Lateinischen Gesengen mit 4 Stimmen* (1603). Text: Matthew 21:9; tr. Frank Stoldt (b. 1958), © 2000 Augsburg Fortress.

"Sing to the Lord" ("Singet dem Herrn ein neues Lied"). Composer: Heinrich Schütz (1585–1672). Source: *Psalmen Davids in Teutzchen Reimen gebracht durch D. Cornelius Berkern* (1628), SWV 196. Text: Cornelius Becker (1561–1604); tr. Martin A. Seltz (b. 1951), © 2000 Augsburg Fortress. Continuo realization: Layton James (b. 1941), © 2000 Augsburg Fortress.

"Sing to the Lord, New Songs Be Raising" ("Chantez à Dieu chanson nouvelle"). Composer: Jan Pieterszoon Sweelinck (1562–1621). Source: *Pseaumes de David nouvellment mis en musique* (1621). Text: Théodore de Bèze (1519–1605); tr. Frank Stoldt (b. 1958), © 2000 Augsburg Fortress.

"Soul, Adorn Yourself with Gladness" ("Schmücke dich, o liebe Seele"). Composer: Friedrich Zipp (b. 1914), © 1956 Bärenreiter-Verlag, Kassel. Reprinted by permission. Tune: SCHMÜCKE DICH, Johann Crüger (1598–1662). Text: Johann Franck (1618–1677); tr. *Lutheran Book of Worship*, © 1978.

"Stay with Us, Lord" ("Bleib bei uns, Herr"). Composer: Michael Praetorius (1571–1621). Source: *Musae Sioniae VIII* (1610). Text: Based on "Ach bleib bei uns, Herr Jesu Christ" (st. 1 and 2), Nürenberg (1611); st. 1: based on *Vespera iam venit* by Philipp Melanchthon (1497–1560); st. 2: Nikoalus Selnecker

(1530–1592); tr. Frank Stoldt (b. 1958), © 2000 Augsburg Fortress.

"The Blood of Jesus Christ" ("Das Blut Jesu Christi"). Composer: Heinrich Schütz (1585–1672). Source: *Kleine Geistliche Konzerte* (1636/1639), SWV 298. Text: 1 John 1:7; tr. Frank Stoldt (b. 1958), © 2000 Augsburg Fortress. Continuo realization: Layton James (b. 1941), © 2000 Augsburg Fortress.

"Then Mary Said to the Angel" ("Dixit Maria ad angelum"). Composer: Hans Leo Hassler (1564–1612). Source: "Missa Dixit Maria," *Missae* (1599). Text: Luke 1:38; tr. composite, © 2000 Augsburg Fortress.

"There Shall a Star Come Out of Jacob" ("Es wird ein Stern aus Jacob aufgeh'n"). Composer: Felix Mendelssohn (1809–1847). Source: *Christus* (incomplete), Opus 97. Tune: WIE SCHÖN LEUCHTET DER MORGENSTERN, Philipp Nicolai (1556–1608). Text: Numbers 24:17; Psalm 2:9; Philipp Nicolai (1556–1608); tr. composite, © 2000 Augsburg Fortress. Organ transcription: Frank Stoldt (b. 1958), © 2000 Augsburg Fortress.

"They that Shall Endure to the End" ("Wer bis an das Ende beharrt"). Composer: Felix Mendelssohn (1809–1847). Source: *Elias* (1846), Opus 70. Text: Matthew 24:13; tr. William Bartholomew (1793–1867), alt.

"To Us Is Born Emmanuel" ("Enatus est Emanuel"). Composer: Michael Praetorius (1571–1621). Source: *Musae Sioniae VI* (1609). Music: Possible contrafacta of anonymous French chanson (c. 1530). Text: Anonymous Latin hymn (c. 1400); tr. Frank Stoldt (b. 1958), © 2000 Augsburg Fortress.

"Today in Triumph Christ Arose" ("Heut triumphieret Gottes Sohn"). Composer: Johann Crüger (1598–1662). Source: *Geistliche Kirchenmelodien* (1649). Tune: HEUT TRIUMPHIERET GOTTES SOHN, Bartholomäus Gesius (c. 1555–1613). Text: Kaspar Stolzhagen (1550–1594); tr. Frank Stoldt (b. 1958), © 2000 Augsburg Fortress.

"We Offer Our Thanks" ("Dank sagen wir alle Gott"). Composer: Heinrich Schütz (1585–1672). Source: *Zwölf Geistliche Gesänge* (1657), SWV 425. Text: Based on Medieval Christmas sequence *Grates nunc omnes reddamus Domino Deo*, attr. Notker Balbus, St. Gall (c. 840–912); tr. Frank Stoldt (b. 1958), © 2000 Augsburg Fortress. Continuo realization: Layton James (b. 1941), © 2000 Augsburg Fortress.

TOPICAL INDEX

PRESENTATION OF OUR LORD
In Peace and Joy I Now Depart, 83

TRANSFIGURATION OF OUR LORD
O Morning Star, How Fair and Bright, 78

LENT
As the Deer, for Water Yearning, 276
For God So Loved the World, 84
God So Loved the World, 88
I Am the Resurrection, 93
We Offer Our Thanks, 247

SUNDAY OF THE PASSION/PALM SUNDAY
A Lamb Goes Uncomplaining Forth, 110
Praise to You, Lord Jesus, 103
Sing Hosanna to the Son of David, 98

HOLY/MAUNDY THURSDAY
Ave verum corpus, 100
O Mighty Word of God Come Down, 214
Praise to You, Lord Jesus, 103
Soul, Adorn Yourself with Gladness, 208

GOOD FRIDAY
A Lamb Goes Uncomplaining Forth, 110
Praise to You, Lord Jesus, 103

EASTER
Arisen Is Our Blessed Lord, 134
Awake, My Heart, with Gladness, 130
I Am the Resurrection, 93
Jesus Christ, My Sure Defense—Alleluia, 117
O Lord, I Trust Your Shepherd Care, 280
O Mighty Word of God Come Down, 214
Sing to the Lord, New Songs Be Raising, 270
Stay with Us, Lord, 132
Today in Triumph Christ Arose, 114

ASCENSION
See God to Heaven Ascending, 137

PENTECOST
Come, Holy Ghost, God and Lord, 140
Creator Spirit, Heavenly Dove, 138
O Spirit of God, Eternal Source, 145

REFORMATION
A Mighty Fortress is Our God, 154
I Build on God's Strong Word, 164
Salvation unto Us Has Come, 146

ALL SAINTS/END TIMES/NOVEMBER
How Lovely Is Thy Dwellingplace, 186
In the Resurrection Glorious, 169
O World So Vain, 184
Rise Up, Rise Up!, 1
They That Shall Endure to the End, 180

THANKSGIVING
Everything You Do, 238
Praise to the Lord, the Almighty, 264
Sing to the Lord, New Songs Be Raising, 270

HOLY BAPTISM
Everything You Do, 238

HOLY COMMUNION
All My Spirit Longs to Savor, 217
Ave verum corpus, 100
O Bread of Life from Heaven, 210
O Lord, I Trust Your Shepherd Care, 280
O Mighty Word of God Come Down, 214
Soul, Adorn Yourself with Gladness, 208
The Blood of Jesus Christ, 202
We Offer Our Thanks, 247

WEDDING
Cantate Domino canticum novum, 287
Everything You Do, 238
Lift Up Your Voice, 282
O Morning Star, How Fair and Bright, 78
Praise to the Lord, the Almighty, 264
Sing to the Lord, 269
Sing to the Lord, New Songs Be Raising, 270

MINISTRY/ORDINATION
Creator Spirit, Heavenly Dove, 138
Everything You Do, 238
How Lovely Are the Messengers, 230
O Spirit of God, Eternal Source, 145
On God Alone My Hope I Build, 258

FUNERAL
How Lovely Is Thy Dwellingplace, 186
I Am the Resurrection, 93
In Peace and Joy I Now Depart, 83
In the Resurrection Glorious, 169
Jesus Christ, My Sure Defense—Alleluia, 117
Let Grief Not Overwhelm You, 220
O Lord, I Trust Your Shepherd Care, 280
O Morning Star, How Fair and Bright, 78
They That Shall Endure to the End, 180

EVENING
My Soul Proclaims the Greatness of the Lord, 11
Now All the Woods Are Sleeping, 262
Stay with Us, Lord, 132

FORGIVENESS
For God So Loved the World, 84
God So Loved the World, 88
The Blood of Jesus Christ, 202

TRUST/HOPE
Grant Peace, We Pray, 250
I Build on God's Strong Word, 164
Jesus Christ, My Sure Defense—Alleluia, 117
Lift Up Your Voice, 282
O Lord, I Trust Your Shepherd Care, 280
On God Alone My Hope I Build, 258
Salvation unto Us Has Come, 146

GENERAL
As the Deer, for Water Yearning, 276
Cantate Domino canticum novum, 287
Everything You Do, 238
Grant Peace, We Pray, 250

INDEX OF BIBLICAL REFERENCES

TUNE INDEX

INDEX OF TEXT SOURCES

INDEX OF TRANSLATIONS

INDEX OF COMPOSERS

TITLE INDEX

ISBN 0-8006-5777-2

90000

9 780800 657772

Augsburg Fortress

12-114

www.augsburgfortress.org